NEW YORK JETS
ALL-TIME GREATS

BY TED COLEMAN

Book design by Jake Slavik
Cover design by Jake Slavik

Photographs ©: Kevin Terrell/AP Images, cover (top), 1 (top); Tony Tomsic/AP Images, cover (bottom), 1 (bottom); Focus on Sport/Getty Images, 4, 7, 8, 14; Rick Stewart/Getty Images Sport/Getty Images, 10; Tom Berg/Getty Images Sport/Getty Images, 13; George Gojkovich/Getty Images Sport/Getty Images, 15, 16; Brian Bahr/Getty Images Sport Classic/Getty Images, 18; Mike Marsland/WireImage/Getty Images, 20

Press Box Books, an imprint of Press Room Editions.

ISBN
978-1-63494-432-8 (library bound)
978-1-63494-449-6 (paperback)
978-1-63494-482-3 (epub)
978-1-63494-466-3 (hosted ebook)

Library of Congress Control Number: 2021916617

Distributed by North Star Editions, Inc.
2297 Waters Drive
Mendota Heights, MN 55120
www.northstareditions.com

Printed in the United States of America
012022

ABOUT THE AUTHOR

Ted Coleman is a sportswriter who lives in Louisville, Kentucky, with his trusty Affenpinscher, Chloe.

TABLE OF CONTENTS

NAMATH
12

CHAPTER 1
GUARANTEED VICTORY

In the 1968 season, the New York Jets made it all the way to the Super Bowl. They were about to face the mighty Baltimore Colts. Most people expected the Colts to win easily. Quarterback **Joe Namath** didn't think people were giving the Jets enough credit. So, he guaranteed that the Jets would win.

STAT SPOTLIGHT

CAREER PASSING YARDS
JETS TEAM RECORD
Joe Namath: 27,057

The Jets did win, 16–7. It was one of the biggest surprises in the history of pro football. However, Namath did much more than win the Super Bowl. In total, he spent 12 seasons with the Jets. He set many team records. And he led the league in passing yards three times.

Receiver **Don Maynard** was Namath's favorite target. Maynard recorded 627 catches during his 13 years with New York. He also gained 11,732 receiving yards and scored 88 touchdowns. All three were team records.

The Jets had a great ground game, too. Running back **Matt Snell** ran for 121 yards in the Super Bowl. He scored the Jets' only touchdown of the game. Snell partnered with running back **Emerson Boozer**. In his 10-year career, Boozer scored 65 touchdowns for the Jets.

MAYNARD
13

Snell and Boozer ran behind an excellent offensive line. Tackle **Winston Hill** led the way. Hill made a name for himself as a strong blocker. He was also reliable. From 1964 to 1976, Hill didn't miss a single game.

PHILBIN
81

8

New York's offense wasn't the only reason the Jets became champions. The team also had a tough defense. In the Super Bowl, the Jets shut down the Colts' passing attack. Linebacker **Larry Grantham** was one of New York's leaders. He had been with the team since 1960. Grantham went on to spend 13 seasons with the Jets.

Defensive end **Gerry Philbin** was known for his physical play. He gave opposing quarterbacks plenty to worry about. He recorded 65 sacks during his nine years with the Jets. However, sacks weren't an official statistic at the time.

CHANGING NAMES

The Jets weren't always called the Jets. In 1960, when they started playing, they were known as the New York Titans. Sonny Werblin took over as the team's new owner in 1963. He planned to move the team to a brand-new stadium. The stadium was very close to an airport. So, Werblin changed the team's name to the Jets.

GASTINEAU

99

CHAPTER 2
NEW YORK SACK EXCHANGE

After winning the Super Bowl, the Jets struggled for most of the 1970s. But in the early 1980s, the team bounced back. The Jets were led by an excellent defensive line. They became known as the "New York Sack Exchange." That's because they brought down opposing quarterbacks so often.

Mark Gastineau was one of the best defensive ends in Jets history. He made the Pro Bowl five years in a row, from 1981 to 1985. One of Gastineau's best seasons came in 1984.

He racked up 22 sacks that year. At the time, it was a National Football League (NFL) record.

Joe Klecko was a boxer before he played in the NFL. He brought his toughness to the Jets' defense. Klecko could play anywhere on the line. In fact, he made the Pro Bowl at three different positions. He was the first player to achieve that.

Marty Lyons was the third member of the "New York Sack Exchange." He spent his entire 11-year career with the Jets. He later became one of the team's radio announcers.

COACHING CAROUSEL

Weeb Ewbank led the Jets for 11 seasons and won 71 games. He left after the 1973 season. Since then, the Jets have struggled to find a good replacement. Only two coaches in team history have winning records. The team hired Robert Saleh in 2021. Jets fans hoped he would be the one to turn things around.

TOON
88

On offense, the Jets had two excellent wide receivers. **Wesley Walker** was legally blind in his left eye. But he still caught 71 touchdown passes in his 13 years with the Jets.

Al Toon joined the team in 1985. In eight years with New York, Toon caught 517 passes. Unfortunately, injuries ended his career early.

McNEIL
24

Tight end **Mickey Shuler** caught at least one pass in 86 straight games. He also hauled in 37 touchdown catches for the Jets. Shuler helped New York reach the playoffs four times in the 1980s.

Freeman McNeil was the team's main running back in the 1980s. In 1982, he led the league with 782 yards. He would have had more, but the season was shortened by a strike. NFL teams played only nine games that year.

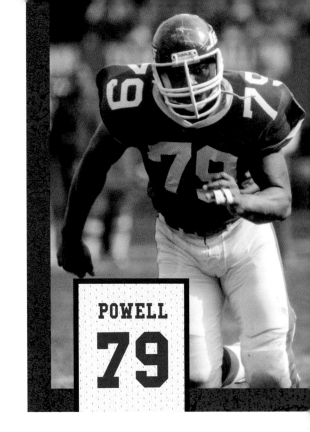

POWELL
79

Marvin Powell was a powerful force on the offensive line. But Powell wasn't just tough. He was also smart. He went to law school in the offseason. And in 1986, he became the president of the NFL Players Union. In that role, he tried to get better working conditions for the league's players.

LEWIS
57

CHAPTER 3
READY FOR TAKEOFF

The Jets struggled for most of the 1990s. But they still had plenty of great players. Linebacker **Mo Lewis** joined the team in 1991. He spent his entire 13-year career with New York. By the time he retired, Lewis had recorded more than 1,200 tackles.

Wayne Chrebet stood 5-foot-10 and weighed only 185 pounds. According to one story, a security guard wouldn't let Chrebet into the team's building. The guard thought Chrebet was too small to be an NFL player.

Chrebet wasn't even drafted when he finished college. Even so, the Jets gave him a

MARTIN
28

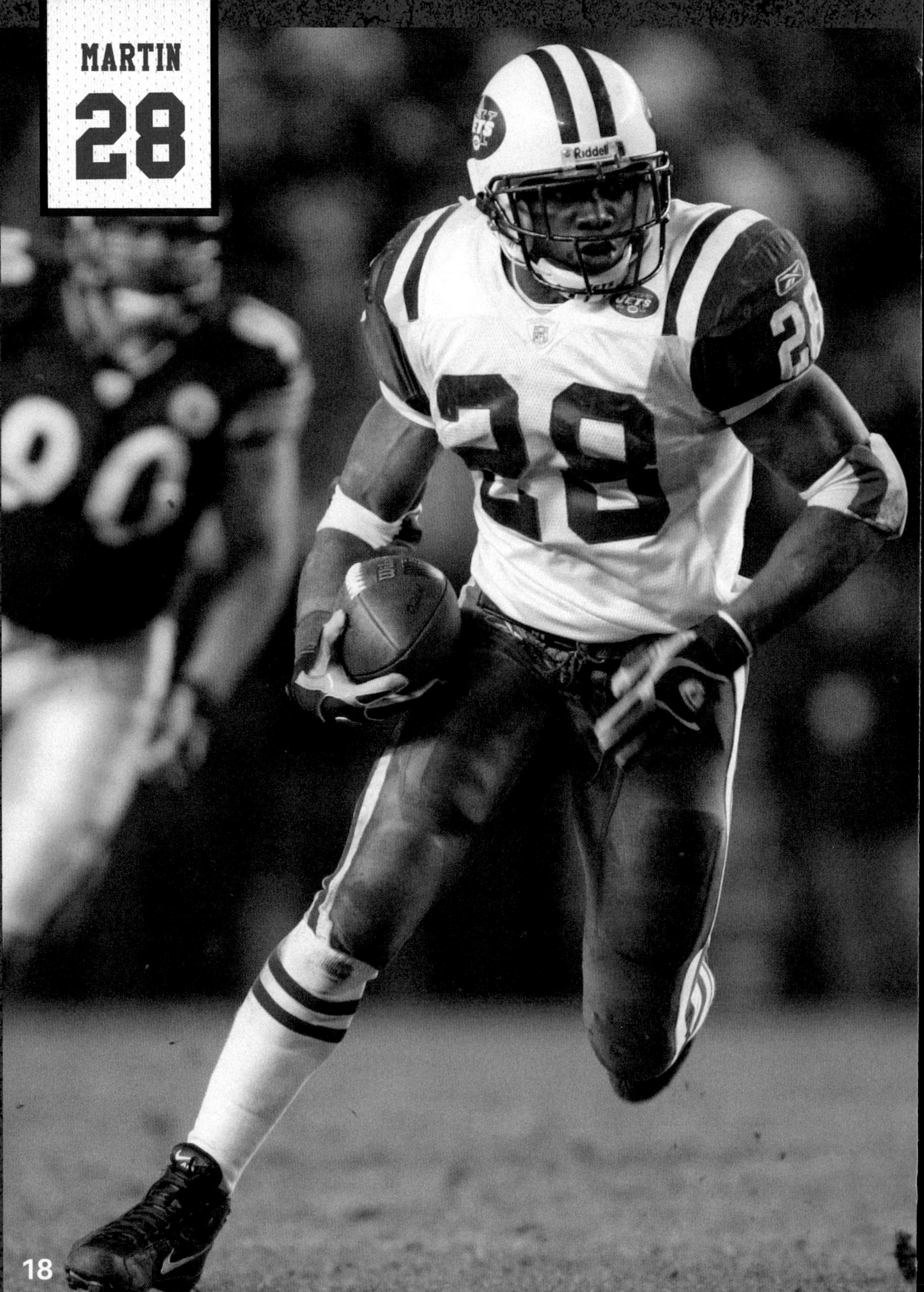

try in 1995. Over the next 11 years, he caught 580 passes. Chrebet may have been small, but he was talented. He became a role model for small players. He was also a favorite of many Jets fans.

Teaming up with Chrebet was running back **Curtis Martin**. In eight years with the Jets, Martin gained more than 10,000 rushing yards. That was a team record. His 58 rushing touchdowns are also a team record.

Martin had an excellent lineman to run behind. Center **Kevin Mawae** made six Pro Bowls in a row from 1999 to 2004. He also ended up in the Hall of Fame.

STAT SPOTLIGHT

CAREER RUSHING YARDS
JETS TEAM RECORD
Curtis Martin: 10,302

REVIS
24

Mawae left the Jets after the 2005 season.
But center **Nick Mangold** was ready to fill
the void. By the late 2000s, Mangold was one
of the best linemen in the league. The Jets
also started to build a winning team. New York

reached the conference title game in the 2009 and 2010 seasons.

Cornerback **Darrelle Revis** was another important part of those playoff teams. Revis didn't have as many interceptions as other great cornerbacks. But that was because few quarterbacks dared to throw the ball his way.

In 2021, the Jets drafted quarterback **Zach Wilson**. He had been one of the best players in college football. Jets fans hoped Wilson would finally be the one to put the team back on top.

QUARTERBACK STRUGGLES

The Jets never had much luck replacing Joe Namath. Quarterback Richard Todd led the team in the late 1970s and early 1980s. However, he threw more interceptions than touchdowns. Ken O'Brien was successful in the 1980s. But he never got the Jets to the Super Bowl. Chad Pennington led New York to the playoffs three times in the 2000s. But like O'Brien, he couldn't get the team to the big game.

TIMELINE

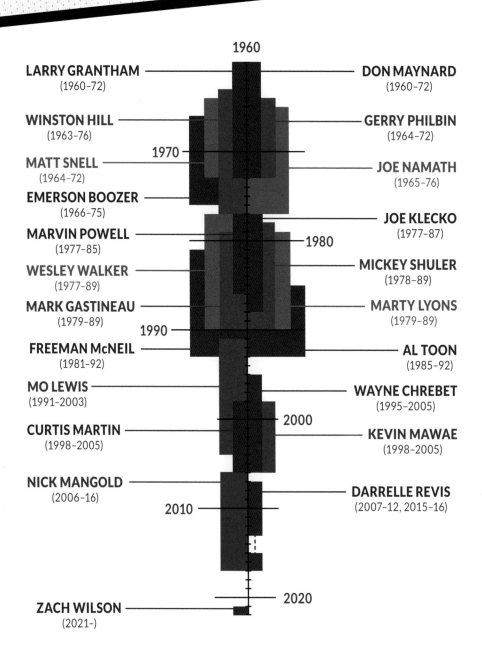

1960

LARRY GRANTHAM
(1960–72)

DON MAYNARD
(1960–72)

WINSTON HILL
(1963–76)

GERRY PHILBIN
(1964–72)

1970

MATT SNELL
(1964–72)

JOE NAMATH
(1965–76)

EMERSON BOOZER
(1966–75)

JOE KLECKO
(1977–87)

MARVIN POWELL
(1977–85)

1980

WESLEY WALKER
(1977–89)

MICKEY SHULER
(1978–89)

MARK GASTINEAU
(1979–89)

MARTY LYONS
(1979–89)

1990

FREEMAN McNEIL
(1981–92)

AL TOON
(1985–92)

MO LEWIS
(1991–2003)

WAYNE CHREBET
(1995–2005)

2000

CURTIS MARTIN
(1998–2005)

KEVIN MAWAE
(1998–2005)

NICK MANGOLD
(2006–16)

DARRELLE REVIS
(2007–12, 2015–16)

2010

2020

ZACH WILSON
(2021–)

NEW YORK JETS

Team history: New York Titans (1960–62), New York Jets (1963–)

Super Bowl titles: 1 (1968)*

Key coaches:

Weeb Ewbank (1963–73), 71–77–6,
1 Super Bowl title

Bill Parcells (1997–99), 29–19–0

Rex Ryan (2009–14), 46–50–0

MORE INFORMATION

To learn more about the New York Jets, go to **pressboxbooks.com/AllAccess**.

These links are routinely monitored and updated to provide the most current information available.

*1966 through 2020

GLOSSARY

conference
A subset of teams within a sports league.

cornerback
A defensive player who covers wide receivers near the sidelines.

linebacker
A player who lines up behind the defensive linemen and in front of the defensive backs.

offensive line
The players who stop defenders from reaching the quarterback and block for running backs.

playoffs
A set of games to decide a league's champion.

Pro Bowl
The NFL's all-star game, in which the league's best players compete.

sack
A tackle of the quarterback behind the line of scrimmage.

strike
When people stop working as a way to demand better pay or better working conditions.

INDEX